Writing Fiction

A HANDBOOK FOR CREATIVE WRITING

Jacqueline Vivelo

WALCH PUBLISHING®

Certified Chain of Custody
Promoting Sustainable
Forest Management

www.sfiprogram.org

SGS-SFI/COC-US09/5501

1   2   3   4   5   6   7   8   9   10

ISBN 0-8251-2308-9

Copyright © 1993
J. Weston Walch, Publisher
P.O. Box 658 • Portland, Maine 04104-0658

Printed in the United States of America

Dedication

*To the students, faculty, and staff of
Council Rock School District,
Bucks County, Pennsylvania,
with thanks for your interest
in creative writing.*

Contents

— CHAPTER 1 —

Expanding Your Creativity:
A Fresh Look at the World

By nature, you and all other humans are already creative, but you can increase your creativity. Because you are unique, you have your own view of life. Your private vision and your point of view are valuable assets in creative writing. Before you begin writing fiction, this chapter will give you an opportunity to take an inventory of your creative awareness, as well as to exercise and encourage your powers of observation.

● *The Creative Personality*

More than thirty years ago, psychologist Frank Barron compiled a list of characteristics of the creative artist. His list included the following:

A. First and above all else, creative people are observant.
B. Creative people see what other people see but also see things other people usually miss.
C. They like pointing out things that might otherwise go unobserved.
D. They think independently.
E. They have more experience than the average person with dreams, fantasy, and imagination.

In this book, you will be encouraged to improve your powers of observation, but just observing isn't enough. You need to share the different, the unusual, the odd things you see.

Michael Ende's *Neverending Story* opens with the logo from the door of a small shop. The words on the door are:

Carl Conrad Coreander
Old Books

Creative people
are observant.

Those words seem ordinary, but in Ende's book the words are printed as mirror writing. The door is glass and the reader is looking from the inside out. A new perspective. You know immediately that you are in for something different. Lewis Carroll also provides a dramatically different perspective in the Alice stories. Whether in Wonderland or through the looking glass, the reader is in a world both like and unlike the ordinary world. Charles Kingsley's main character in *Water Babies* lives for a time under the sea, an experience that changes not only his point of view but his whole life.

Not every book or story takes such drastically altered perspectives, but every writer needs a fresh point of view, one that is his or hers alone.

● *Changing Your Perspective*

Try this experiment in class for an actual change in perspective. Shift the angle of your desk, or change your place to get a different view of the room. You might, for instance, sit on the floor, stand up, reverse your desk, or tilt your head backwards so that you are looking at the ceiling. Hold that position for three minutes of silent observation. Really *look*. Notice every detail that is available to you. Think of how you can describe the details to someone else. Perhaps you see a stain on the ceiling tile or a crack in the floor. Examine the shape of the stain or the crack. Is the stain in the shape of South America? Does the crack look like Abraham Lincoln's nose in profile?

When time is up, compare what you observed with the observations of other class members. Do the comments of others give you ideas for additional things you might have looked for?

Think of a way that you could have a character change his or her perspective, either for a moment within the story (as in looking through the wrong side of a glass door with words on it) or for the entire story (as in living on the other side of a mirror or under the sea).

You might have a character hide on top of a tall cabinet, from which the room is seen in a different way. You could send your character into space, a foreign country, or another time. Share your ideas and compare them with those of other class members.

● *Exercises in Creative Thinking*

1. One of the pleasures of writing is being able to name everything—people, cities, streets, animals. Your story is your own world. You can give whatever names you like within that world. For each category below suggest several names. Try for five each.

    Avoid names that are already attached to the category. You could name a race horse Gone with the Wind, but don't call it Man O' War. Man O' War has his place in history. You might call a clown Slow Joe, but don't call him Bozo. Your goal is originality.

    Race horse _____

    Clown _____

    TV show _____

    Cartoon hero _____

    Dog or cat _____

    Restaurant _____

2. Good writers often take old phrases or clichés and give them new twists. Try doing that with the expressions below. Your first thought will probably be too obvious. "As quick as" may make you think of lightning, or a wink, or a jack rabbit. Think again for a less obvious answer.

    as quick as _____   as slow as _____

    as high as _____   as wide as _____

    as smart as _____   as dumb as _____

    as safe as _____   as old as _____

    as rich as _____   as poor as _____

    as hungry as _____   as big as _____

    Notice that changing an old expression makes you see things in a new way.

3. How many ways can a brick be used? Most people might stop after two or three suggestions. After all, you can use a brick in a building

or use it as a doorstop. What reasonable person could do more? Creative thinkers have suggested *dozens* of uses for the ordinary brick. These include using it as a bookend, a paperweight, a prop for an uneven table, a weight for something you want to sink in the river, a toy, a nutcracker, a decoration (after it has been painted), a weapon, exercise equipment (as both a weight to lift and a step for aerobic exercise), ballast for a boat, an anchor for a small boat, a prop for a window with a broken sash, a seat for a doll, a cooking surface in a campfire—and the list goes on.

Putting yourself in your most creative frame of mind, make a list of all the uses you can think of for the following objects: potato, book, pencil. If you think you can only write with the pencil, read the book, or cook the potato, your imagination is in need of exercise. Make a master list for each of the objects, combining all the suggestions your class can think of.

● *The Magic of Metaphors*

Metaphors are comparisons that allow you to explain much in few words. "Time is but the stream I go a-fishing in," Thoreau said, managing to put several paragraphs of meaning into one sentence. Explain these metaphors:

Truth is a hard deer to hunt.
The snow was a pillow, a featherbed all
  around me.
His mind is an unweeded garden.

His mind is an unweeded garden.

1. Restricting yourself to a type of food, describe what life is like and include a brief explanation. For instance, "Life is a plate of spaghetti, awkward to handle and sometimes embarrassing, but worth the trouble." Or, "Life is a watermelon, sweet and juicy, but full of annoying little things that get in the way of your pleasure."

2. Next, compare life to anything that isn't food. You don't want to say "Life is a jungle." Come up with your own comparison.

3. Finally, with no restrictions, except a request that you try for something original, make up a metaphor for "school."

● *The Wonderful World of "What If . . . ?"*

In an ordinary, everyday frame of mind, you may look at a situation and say, "So, that's how it is." In a creative frame of mind, you could look at the same situation and say, "That's how it is *now*, but what if. . .?" Imagination takes over and reshapes the familiar world.

What if people lived backwards, starting life old and wrinkled and growing younger and younger until we faded away?

What if you had a closet in your room that was really a time-travel capsule?

What if grades in school were awarded randomly—say, by lottery or by picking them out of a hat?

What if you suddenly found yourself totally alone in Times Square and discovered you were the only living thing in New York City?

What if our atmosphere became poisoned and we had to live underground?

What if children were forced to leave their families at age twelve to take care of themselves and make their own way in life?

What if dogs could talk?

What if schools, stores, businesses all ran on a 24-hour schedule, with some of us going to school from eight to four, some from four to midnight, and some from midnight to eight in the morning?

What if people were all different colors?

What if human beings had fur, as most mammals do?

1. What results do you imagine for each situation above? How could each one be turned into a story?

2. Take a moment to think up your own "what if." Nothing is a wrong answer. Nothing is too absurd.

● *Creative Problem-Solving*

One of the characteristics of a writer is an ability to find unusual solutions to the difficulties the characters in a story face. Try your imagination on the following problems. Don't discard an idea just because it sounds outrageous. Ideas that seem silly at first glance can be made workable. A few ridiculous ideas may be the boost your imagination needs. Here are your problems. Suggest as many solutions as you can imagine.

Problems

How could you get away?

1. An essential piece of evidence is locked inside a waterproof, unbreakable box. No key is available. How will you retrieve the piece of evidence without destroying it along with the box?

2. You are a guest at a large country house where you are expected to appear in a costume for the party that evening. Your luggage was lost, including your Egyptian outfit. You can't ask your host or one of the other guests for a costume. What will you wear?

3. A gang of international kidnappers have locked you into a room. You are tied to the bedpost, and a guard is posted outside the door of your room, which is on the third floor of the building. How could you get away?

4. One morning you wake up, stumble into the bathroom, and glance into the mirror to find you are looking at a totally unfamiliar face. You look nothing at all like you usually look. How can you explain the situation?

5. You are visiting at a large farmhouse belonging to distant relatives. While you are out walking, you meet an impressive old gentleman who talks to you for half an hour. Later that evening when you tell your relatives about the man you met, they tell you that he sounds just like old Mr. Sanderson, who died twenty years ago. Without resorting to the supernatural, explain who the man really was and why your relatives were mistaken.

How good were your solutions to the problems? Did you enjoy some of the problems more than others? Compare your solutions with those of others in the class to see how much variety you can find.

Through working on these five problems, you have begun to plan stories and develop plots. You may even want to use one of the above situations to write your own short story. With your own characters, your own twists to the plot, and your original ending, the story becomes yours. No matter how many people start from the same idea, you may each end up with a different, original story.

● *Keep Exercising Your Creativity*

The end of the chapter should not mean the end of exercising your imagination. Each chapter that follows contains some opportunities to stretch your imagination.

With more thought you can always come up with one more idea. Above all, look for the fun in creative writing. Keep in mind that "If you're writing as a chore, what you write may be a bore." Write to please yourself. Write for the fun of it. Go courageously in search of ideas that are uniquely yours.

— CHAPTER 2 —

Collecting Story Ideas:
Stories Wherever You Look

Story ideas are everywhere. Once you begin looking for ideas and collecting them, you'll find yourself adding several possibilities to your list each day. **Do** begin a list. Even though you know you'll never write all the stories you think of, it's good to have many possibilities to choose from each time you decide to work on a story. Later on, you may find yourself combining several ideas to write one story.

Where do we begin finding ideas?

● *Stories from Life*

Real life can be a source of story ideas if you can separate your storytelling from a need to relate the incident "the way it really happened." Think of it this way: fiction gives you a chance to make real-life adventures more exciting, more dangerous. Fiction also gives you a chance to change the way things turned out in reality.

Begin by making a list of several incidents you remember vividly. Don't worry about relating the whole incident at this point. Just note enough details to remind yourself of this particular experience later. For instance, your list might look like these student examples:

1. The day we rescued the cat from the well.

2. When Tony and I found the skull in the woods.

3. Putting the pig on the roof.

The day we rescued the cat from the well

9

Just reading through this list may suggest story possibilities to you. Your imagination is bound to supply details that may be far removed from the events recalled by the original student.

When you have a similar list, choose one experience and write a detailed description of the event as it really occurred.

The student whose list is given above wrote about the day she and her friend Tony found the skull of a rabbit in the woods near their neighborhood. Since the skull was complete with a full set of teeth, Tony retrieved a tube of "Colgate with fluoride," while the author contributed "Dad's toothbrush" so the pair could brush the long-preserved teeth.

Writing first about real life can help to remind us to include specific details. Note that naming the brand of toothpaste makes better (and funnier) reading than just using the word "toothpaste." The author might also have said only that she brought a toothbrush from home. How much better it is to know that it was her father's toothbrush. Fiction can always profit from details from life.

Now that you've made your list, chosen one memory, and written a brief recollection from the past, look again at the real experience with the intention of turning it into fiction. Nothing very dramatic happened as a result of the student's discovery of the rabbit's skull. So let's apply imagination. What if—

1. Having collected toothpaste and toothbrush, the two friends turn on an outside hydrant to clean the skull and its teeth.

2. Excited over their find, they forget to turn off the water when they finish.

3. The father of the narrator comes home and falls in the mudslide the two have created.

4. Already angry, he pursues the matter until he discovers the full truth—bones, toothbrush, and all.

The story began from fact, but now it is more fiction than truth.

You don't need to write a complete story. Just come up with a series of imaginary events that use one real memory as their starting point.

● *Starting with a Title*

Titles can suggest stories to us. You should collect phrases for possible use as titles. Some titles seem to leap off the page, implying more than the words say.

Even when people use the same title, they write very different stories. A group of twenty students given the title "An Eye to the Wind" came up with twenty individual ideas. Here, in brief, are two of those ideas:

1. "An Eye to the Wind" is the story of a man who stands in a special place during storms and looks into the wind. Watching the wind he can see the future unfold. Because he sees what's to come, he is the adviser or councilor for his country.

2. "An Eye to the Wind" is the story of a girl of about 13 who's a member of a troubled family. In the story she is just coming to realize that she has to plot her own course in life, make her way independently of her parents.

Both ideas suggest intriguing, though completely different, stories.

Before you try the exercise below, compare your imagination with other class members by having everyone suggest a story for the same title. Suppose we try the title, "Where Dragons Walk." Take a moment quietly to see what ideas come to you. Then share your story possibility with the class. You'll find new ideas coming to you as you listen to the ideas of the rest of the class. Note your own ideas and any others that have strong appeal for you.

Where Dragons Walk

Now try this exercise for yourself, knowing that you can go on to use the titles you choose to write complete stories. Titles don't belong to anyone and may be used over and over.

Imagine that the list of titles that follows is the index in a collection of stories. Choose a title that interests you and then imagine you are reading (not writing) the story. What is the story about? Note the title of your choice and write a brief description of the story. Follow the same procedure for a second and then a third title. Does one of the ideas have a strong appeal for you? Can you imagine the characters, sketch them out? Add these story ideas to your list of possibilities.

Titles

Sky Song
Wait for Me
You Gotta Die Laughing
Purple Magic
Playing the Game
Shooting Star
King of the Hill
Look Before You Leap
What Danny Knew
Paper Sack
Crossword Clue
Before Dark
How Many Clocks?
Ears to the Blind
Involving Daytime
Escape

● *Ideas from a Beginning Sentence*

Suppose someone gave you a beginning for a story. Could you finish it?

Yes, of course. You probably do it all the time. Consider a book you read recently. Didn't you find yourself guessing ahead, thinking, "I bet I know what's going to happen"? Or, saying "I hope such-and-such doesn't happen"? In the middle of an exciting movie, have you found yourself thinking or perhaps saying out loud, "There's someone hiding behind that door"? If you have ever guessed ahead of the action of a movie or story, you have engaged in plot development.

Choose one of the beginnings that follow and write a short description of the story as you think it should unfold. (No stories are "right" or "wrong" continuations of the beginning. The purpose is to be original and to discover a story idea that is uniquely yours.)

● *Beginning Sentences*

1. Red Starks was a found child and never had a mother or father that was ever heard of.

2. "I'm going to be late," Maggie complained. "You always ruin everything!"

3. The river used to be the first thing we'd see when we came to Juniper, but the new road comes in from another direction.

4. "I've either had a nightmare," Mark told me, "or else I saw a ghost last night."

5. The book, a small red square with gold hinges, was not like any I had ever seen, and I was sure it hadn't been there the day before.

6. The last egg rolled off the counter before I had a chance to catch it, and that was when I knew I would have to answer for what had happened that afternoon.

7. Not a night went by without Damon's seeing at least one fire on the distant hills that he, in his isolation, knew he would never reach.

8. The Christmas I was sixteen we were snowbound at my uncle's farm.

● *Exercises for Collecting Story Ideas*

By now you should have several story ideas in your notebook. Keep them. Keep track of all your ideas. Even the ones that seem weak when they first occur to you may become part of a more complex story later. Many things in everyday life can spark ideas for writing. Here are some specific things you can do to build your list:

1. Keep a dream diary. Many stories have begun as dreams. Keep a small notepad by your bed and write down whatever you can remember from your dreams each morning. Don't be discouraged if you go for several days without recalling anything from your dreams. Begin your diary by writing down summaries of any noteworthy dreams from the past.

2. Go through a newspaper with the objective of finding at least three story possibilities. Notice photos as well as articles. Don't overlook the classified ads as sources.

3. As a class project, bring in photos cut from magazines. Pool the contributions and take one at random. Examine the picture and think of a story to go with it. Share your ideas in class and try trading pictures.

4. Pick a single emotion—anger, love, pity, jealousy, or whatever—and think of a story idea to reflect that emotion.

Go through a newpaper to find story ideas.

5. Decide how you would write a modern version of a well-known fairy tale, updating the characters and the setting. Describe how you would alter the events to make them contemporary.

CHAPTER 3

Finding Characters:
All the Strangers in Your Mind

From real-life experience, from movies and television, from reading, and from our imagination, each of us has collected a mixed assortment of characters. Try imagining that you have enough characters in your head to populate a fair-sized town. Because they have been shaped by your own view of the world, your individual experiences, these characters are unique, each one a little different from any character that has ever appeared in fiction.

You don't need to write about your favorite character from fiction. You have your own characters—many of them—to choose from for the stories you will write.

The task now is to get to know some of these characters better, to bring them into focus, and to select a few to write about. You'll find that as you move characters out of the imaginary town in your mind and into the shared world of fiction, new characters will keep showing up.

Sometimes a story will begin when you find yourself thinking, "What a great idea for a plot!" At other times the desire to write comes when you think up a character too good to lose. If an idea for a plot occurs to you first, thinking through the development of the story may give you definite ideas for the characters who will take part in it. On the other hand, strong characters may help you to imagine the sort of situations they will be involved in, assisting in plot development.

● *Characters from Imagination*

To discover a character who already exists in your own imagination, try writing answers to the following questionnaire. Working rapidly, write down the answers that come to you. Don't give answers that apply to yourself, and don't try to describe any particular person. Give random replies. When you've answered all the questions, read back through the list to discover what character you've created. The character should appeal to you. After all, it came from your imagination.

Character Profile

Answer the following questions quickly. Often your first thought will be the best. Don't try to describe a person you already have in mind. The purpose is to discover a new personality.

1. Is your character male or female? _____

2. How old is the character? _____

3. What is the color of hair? _____

    Eyes? _____ Skin? _____

4. Describe your character's physical appearance and body type:

    _____

    _____

    _____

    _____

5. Describe the character's voice and any favorite words or expressions:

    _____

    _____

    _____

6. How is this character dressed? What style clothing would he/she

    usually wear?_____

    _____

    _____

7. Mention any special characteristics, quirks, or physical traits that

    would make your character memorable: _____

    _____

    _____

8. How intelligent is this character? Mention whether or not the character has common sense, special talents or abilities: _____

_____

_____

_____

9. What is the character's general attitude toward life? (Happy? Carefree? Worried? Rebellious?) _____

_____

10. What sort of family does your character come from? _____

_____

_____

_____

11. Name and briefly describe friends and acquaintances of your character:

_____

_____

_____

12. Where was this character born? _____

13. Where does the character live? _____

14. Describe the character's neighborhood and house: _____

_____

_____

_____

15. What is the time period of the story? (If the story does not take place in the present, be specific about which historical era or time in the future is involved.) _____

_____

_____

16. List interests or hobbies of the character: _____

_____

_____

17. What is the character's goal or ambition? _____

_____

_____

18. Mention at least one major event in the character's life: _____

_____

_____

***

Pause now and read over the information above. Does an image of a character emerge? Try to give your character a fitting name.

19. Name: _____

20. What nicknames could be given to your character? _____

_____

_____

So now you have pulled a character out of your imagination. Maybe this is a character you will want to think about, perhaps write about. In any case, you can use the questionnaire over and over. Even when you come up with a character in other ways, you may want to return to the questions to help develop details, or just to be sure you know your character very well before you begin to write.

● *Characters from Real Life*

One way to create an original character is to begin with someone you know. While it isn't a good idea to put actual people into your stories, real people may provide possibilities for fictional development.

You can begin by turning yourself into a fictional character. Try these exercises:

1. Write a 200-word description of a character who is just like you—except twenty years older. Give your character a job, family, home, and lifestyle that might be yours in the future.

2. Move yourself backward in time—to the early days in this country or to another era in some other country. (For example, pioneering days in America, wartime in Germany, the days of the pharaohs in Egypt, the period when pirates sailed the seas.) Who would you be? What kind of life would you live? Describe not only yourself, but the time, place, and life-style you envision for yourself.

Picture yourself as a character in the days when pirates sailed the seas.

By this time you have probably grasped the secret behind using real people as characters. You use them only *as starting points*. Try these exercises:

3. Use your brother, sister, or a friend as a starting point and describe an *animal* character who has some characteristics of the real-life model you've chosen.

4. Use a photograph (avoiding celebrities) from a newspaper or book. Describe the person, supplying characteristics and details of his or her life from your imagination.

5. Write a sketch of a favorite character in fiction. Why do you like this character? Which do you find more appealing, the personality of the character or the adventures experienced by the character? Imagine the character in a situation of your own devising. Summarize the adventure you have envisioned for this character.

● *Finding a Hero*

In a work of fiction, the central character is called the hero or heroine, without implying any special qualities or superiority. Another term for the central character is *protagonist*. Regardless of which term is used, this character is the focal point of the story and deserves individual consideration.

With some writing experience, you will discover that you can make a wide variety of characters the protagonists in your stories, but most writers find it easiest to start with a character who is very similar to the writer. In that case, your central character may be your alter ego, your other self.

On the other hand, don't overlook the benefits that come from working with a protagonist who is completely unlike you. Gaining distance from your main character can have a positive effect on your writing. Try working with a main character who is an opposite to you in some way.

● *Exercises in Developing a Protagonist*

1. Write a detailed description of something that has happened to you in the last few days. The incident does not need to be significant or exciting. You might begin with the sound of the alarm this morning and describe getting dressed, eating breakfast, and leaving the house. Describe yourself objectively, and do not write in the first person. Use details from your own day but imagine that the character is about to face a major crisis far removed from the reality of your own recent past.

2. Imagine a character who is very different from you—someone of the opposite sex, someone much older or younger, someone of a different race, someone from another country. Write a few paragraphs taking the character step by step through some daily experience, such as eating dinner, going home from work or school, preparing for bed.

3. When you have completed both the exercises above, answer and discuss the following questions:

    (a) Do you find it easier to write about a character who is like you or one who is different?

    (b) How do you feel about the two different characters?

    (c) Which one appeals to your imagination more?

Create a villain of your own.

● *A Villain of Your Own*

Villains are among the most memorable characters in fiction—Dracula, Darth Vader, Simon Legree. We know their names even if we don't know their stories. Before you create your own villain, discuss these questions with a small group or with the entire class: Who are your favorite villains? Why do you like them? Which evil females of fiction do you remember? What makes a "great" villain?

After discussion with the group, work on your own or with no more than one or two other people to create a villain. What characteristics make him or her objectionable? What is your villain's greatest strength? Give the villain at least one attractive characteristic (good looks, strong intellect, physical prowess, etc.). Write a full page of nerve-tingling description.

● *Additional Activities*

1. Write a five-hundred-word biography of a character, incorporating physical, emotional, mental, and social characteristics such as those asked for in the Character Profile earlier in this chapter.

2. Create an animal character, using distinctive traits to make your non-human character unforgettable.

3. Imagine you are going to write about a character who is facing a major change in his or her life: a move to another state, a change in schools, the death of a relative or pet, sudden wealth—or any other dramatic change for better or worse. Then answer the following questions: Who is your character (name, age, sex, etc.)? What is the change the character faces? How does he or she feel about the transition? Is one emotion dominant or does the character have mixed feelings? What problems does the change pose? What good may come from the change? What is the worst that may happen as a result of the change?

4. Write a two-page dialogue between yourself and a character. Begin like this:

    Me: Who are you?

    Character: My name is _____.

    Move back and forth between yourself and the character until you have a clear idea who he or she is.

5. Imagine two characters who are opposites in their approach to a problem. Picture the two sitting facing each other. Make up a conversation between them in which each explains why he or she is different from the other. (For example, one might defend his cautious approach, while the other might defend his boldness.)

6. Write a one-page description of a hero. Remember to give him or her a weakness, as well as plenty of admirable characteristics.

7. Discuss the following names. Which sound older? Richer? Which might be main characters? Which could be villains? Which ones ones sound comic? Choose two or three of the names from the list and write one paragraph for each describing the character the name suggests to you:

David Megaro	Benjamin Bonowitz
Fuzzy Weller	Cappy Hoskins
Mary Elizabeth Fisher	Tiffany Cathcart
Abigail Burridge	Matilda Von Crawn
Harry Longenecker	Clarence Pilcher
Tilly Tolliver	Zachary Tombs
Ned Dunkle	Patty Forbes
Louise Sharp	Horace Gummidge

8. Think of two or three names on your own and write a short description for each. Try for variety, such as a comic character, a hero, a bully, a snob.

● *Character Roundup*

By now you should have a good-sized collection of characters. You may never use them all in stories, but thinking about them and finding ways to make them individual will help you as you create new characters.

As a final exercise, choose one or more of the characters you've thought up while working on this chapter, and write a short scene featuring the character(s) of your choice. Of course, something must *happen*, but don't worry too much about plot at this point. Just give your characters a chance to get into action.

— CHAPTER 4 —

Plotting the Story:
What Happens Next?

If you don't have a problem, you don't have a story.

Stop for a moment and silently repeat the sentence. Now close your eyes and picture a white screen with that first sentence printed across it in large bold letters.

IF YOU DON'T HAVE A PROBLEM, YOU DON'T HAVE A STORY.

One day Elizabeth Overby, who was young, beautiful, and healthy, tossed her soft curls and laughed up at the clear blue sky as she and her friend Jim Miller set off to bike around Fancher Lake. In the carriers attached to their bikes the pair had turkey sandwiches, grapes, peaches, soda, and two large pieces of carrot cake for the lunch they planned to share when they reached Pemberton's Point.

Picnic under the trees

If our two healthy, happy young people have a delightful picnic under the trees, if the fair weather holds for the day, if they laugh and talk without a cross word, if the bikes keep rolling on smooth ground with no breakdowns—if *no* mishaps occur, they'll have a great day but no one will have a story.

No matter how unfair it sounds, the inescapable fact of storytelling is that your characters must face obstacles or difficulties of some sort. On the other hand, if you have always believed that a story plot was some mysterious thing available only to special people, you can relax.

23

Reconsider Elizabeth and Jim and their bike ride on a beautiful day. What might go wrong? Take a moment to list possibilities.

Perhaps a sudden wind will capsize a boat on the lake; only Elizabeth and Jim are around to rescue the lone sailor who was struck on the head by the boat's edge.

Or, in the middle of their picnic the young people overhear screams and catch sight of someone being abducted.

Or, Jim's bike hits a rock and he is injured in a fall. Unable to walk, with a storm approaching, he must join his ingenuity with Elizabeth's skills to find a way to get him back home.

You will have other ideas. Share them and develop new ideas by combining possibilities.

Consider these one-sentence plot summaries of classic novels:

A large, gentle dog is taken from the family where he's a much-loved pet and is sold as a sled dog to face life in a harsh and often cruel new environment. (Jack London's *Call of the Wild*)

Jim Hawkins ships out as cabin boy aboard a boat on which most of the crew turn out to be pirates who mutiny under the leadership of Long John Silver so they can claim a hidden treasure for themselves. (Robert Louis Stevenson's *Treasure Island*)

When word comes that her father has died, leaving her penniless, Sara Crewe goes from being a pampered rich girl in a private school to a drudge at the mercy of the hard-hearted woman who directs the school. (Frances H. Burnett's *Little Princess*)

A young male crosses a boundary into territory strictly forbidden to him and finds himself pursued by an angry landowner who intends to shoot the intruder. (Beatrix Potter's *Tale of Peter Rabbit*)

A noted detective tries to rid a family of the curse involving a huge, hound-like fiend that has brought unexpected death for several generations. (Sir Arthur Conan Doyle's *Hound of the Baskervilles*)

When Fiver convinces Hazel and the others that their home will be destroyed, the whole group sets off on a perilous adventure. (Richard Adams's *Watership Down*)

If Buck had lived out his life as a family pet, the only call he'd be answering would be "Come and get it" when his supper was ready, a good life for a dog but not much of a story.

If Long John Silver had been Jim's good pal and the loyal mate he pretended to be, Jim could still have had the thrill of discovering lost treasure, but he wouldn't have had a chance to become a hero.

If Sara Crewe's father hadn't disappeared, the small variations in her daily routine wouldn't have been worth recording in print.

If Peter had minded his mother and stayed out of Farmer McGregor's garden, he would have been spared the chamomile tea, but we would have lost one of the most exciting chase tales of early childhood.

If Sherlock Holmes had scoffed at the idea of demons and curses, he could have avoided the damp chill of the moors—but a challenge ignored doesn't make a story.

If Fiver had not believed in his vision of the future or if the other rabbits had rejected his prediction, they might have been destroyed. While a story may end in the death or destruction of the main characters (as in the case of *Frankenstein* or *The Strange Case of Dr. Jekyll and Mr. Hyde*), destruction alone doesn't make much of a story. As readers, our attention is caught by the contest, the struggle against defeat.

Changes, betrayals, losses, misfortunes—stories are made of the tough things in life.

Below are some steps to finding a plot. Just as we can reuse the format for developing a character, you can return to these steps to work out as many plots as you like. But let's begin by concentrating on just one idea.

● *Steps to Finding a Plot*

1. On the basis of your background, experience, area of interest, what kind of story would you like to write? (Mystery? Love story? Science fiction? Adventure?)

2. What sort of character would you like to have in your story?

3. What sort of problem would a character like this face in this kind of story? What obstacle is he or she up against? What ambition matters so much that he or she is willing to struggle for it?

4. What odds does the character have to overcome? What predicaments does he or she face? Does the main character have competitors or face a villain in the story?

5. In one sentence express your character's aim and the problems that stand between the character and what she hopes to achieve.

● *Complicating the Plot*

Because every plot needs a few complications, let's take a moment to look at some problems and decide how they can be made worse than they already are.

Suppose your character Megan Phillips is sitting quietly behind a column in the art museum sketching a statue when she overhears a plan to steal a famous painting.

Complicate your plot.

Her pleasant day of drawing has been interrupted in an unexpected way. Good start for a story. Now can you think of a way to complicate the problem facing her?

Suppose the theft is being planned so that the blame will fall on the director of the museum, who is Megan's father. Now Megan has to save the painting and protect her father.

Or, suppose the plotters spot Megan at the last minute and guess that she may have heard their plan. Now Megan has to escape from the thieves and find a way to stop the theft.

Look at each character's dilemma and say, "Yes, that's bad, but what if. . . ." Don't add a new problem. Take the existing problem and make it worse.

Try supplying complications for each of the following situations:

1. Bill Morice has been picked for the lead in the school play even though he suffers from stage fright and forgets his lines when he's in front of a group.

2. The Hunter family has just moved into their "new" house when Polly finds that the house is already occupied—by a ghost.

3. This year is to be just one more in a series of great successes for Marcia Ridley, until Pamela Grover transfers to Marcia's school. First Marcia loses her place on the swim team to Pamela, and that's just the beginning of her troubles.

4. Nothing could be better than a semester in France as an exchange student—unless it's a trip home just before Christmas. The semester has ended and Alec Bremmer is on his way home when he gets separated from his group and misses the plane.

5. Anne Jackson thinks it's fun to dress like her friend Laura, since the two girls look so much alike, until she finds herself kidnapped by mistake.

6. Working for his uncle isn't Peter's favorite summer job, but the pay is good. But no pay can make up for the danger when Peter discovers that something more complicated than wood is being shipped from the lumberyard.

7. "I hate you, Bootsie. You're going to suffer," reads the note that Barbara finds on her desk. Who wrote it? Was it even meant for her? Nobody has called her "Bootsie" in more than five years.

8. "It's the second time a local store has been robbed overnight with no signs of anyone breaking in," Gary told his friend Chad. "The police don't have a clue, but I think we can solve the thefts."

[Note that sometimes characters may *choose* the problem they face within the story.]

● *Story Setup*

Refer to the list of story ideas you have been developing since Chapter 2 and choose one to use in the following exercise. Don't turn this into a long or agonizing choice. You can always go back and pick a different idea if you don't like the way your first choice is developing. One key to writing is to **be flexible**. Let your own creativity guide you.

Working from the idea you already have in mind, develop brief descriptions for the following story elements. Jot down whatever comes to mind; you can revise later.

A. Situation _____

_____

_____

B. Problem _____

_____

_____

(a) Complication _____

_____

_____

(b) Surprise _____

_____

_____

(c) Additional complication _____

_____

_____

(d) Asset of main character (for dealing with the problem)

_____

_____

(e) Complication that calls for speed _____

_____

_____

(f) Resolution _____

_____

Once you have an idea (or situation) for a story, you need to add characters and then you need to present those characters with a problem that fits the situation you've chosen. Developing the plot means elaborating the problem. If you have successfully completed the form above, you've outlined a plot.

— CHAPTER 5 —

Creating a Setting:
The Here and Now of the Story

Creating a setting means helping a reader to "see" the time and place in which the story's action occurs. Nouns and verbs are often more helpful than adjectives. Look at the beginnings of the following stories:

In the ancient city of London, on a certain autumn day in the second quarter of the sixteenth century, a boy was born to a poor family of the name of Canty, who did not want him.

> Mark Twain, *The Prince and the Pauper*

The story had held us, round the fire, sufficiently breathless, but except the obvious remark that it was gruesome, as on Christmas eve in an old house a strange tale should essentially be, I remember no comment uttered till somebody happened to note it as the only case he had met in which such a visitation had fallen on a child.

> Henry James, *The Turn of the Screw*

On a fine warm evening in late summer, over a hundred years ago, a boy might have been seen leading a donkey across Southwark Bridge in the city of London.

> Joan Aiken, *Black Hearts in Battersea*

Each of these excerpts just happens to be an opening sentence. All three place the reader at once in time and locale. You also learn something of atmosphere and have some hint of the story to come, whether it concerns an unwanted child, a gruesome tale, or a young man with a donkey.

Setting locates your story in time and space.

Knowing where you are in terms of both time and space helps you to follow the action of a story.

Developing a habit of observation, collecting settings, and recording descriptions are good things to do when you can't decide which story to write next.

● *Settings Crucial to the Story*

Some stories may take place almost anywhere. If setting doesn't matter, description of the setting should be limited. Sometimes, however, setting may be so important that it almost assumes the role of a character in the story. Just as the high seas and the pirate ships are necessary to *Captain Blood*, the frozen tundra is essential to *White Fang*. Note how the authors set the scene in the two examples below:

Yesterday afternoon set in misty and cold. I had half a mind to spend it by my study fire, instead of wading through heath and mud to Wuthering Heights. On coming up from dinner, however . . . , on mounting the stairs with this lazy intention, and stepping into the room, I saw a servant girl on her knees surrounded by brushes and coal-scuttles, and raising an infernal dust as she extinguished the flames with heaps of cinders. This spectacle drove me back immediately; I took my hat, and, after a four-miles' walk, arrived at Heathcliff's garden gate just in time to escape the first feathery flakes of a snow shower.

On that bleak hill top the earth was hard with a black frost, and the air made me shiver through every limb. Being unable to remove the chain, I jumped over, and running up the flagged causeway bordered with straggling gooseberry bushes, knocked vainly for admittance, till my knuckles tingled and the dogs howled.

Emily Brontë, *Wuthering Heights*

In *Wuthering Heights*, the Yorkshire moors become a major part of the story. The harshness and isolation of the moors are a match for the uncultured, lonely Heathcliff.

Two or three days and nights went by; I reckon I might say they swum by, they slid along so quiet and smooth and lovely. Here is the way we put in the time. It was a monstrous big river down there—sometimes a mile and half wide; we run nights, and laid up and hid daytimes; soon as night was most gone we stopped navigating and tied up—nearly always in the dead water under a towhead; and then cut young cottonwoods and willows, and hid the raft with them. Then we set out the lines. Next we slid into the river and had a swim, so as to freshen up and cool off; then we set down on the sandy bottom where the water was about knee deep, and watched the daylight come. Not a sound anywheres—perfectly still—just like the whole world was asleep, only sometimes the bullfrogs a-cluttering, maybe. The first thing to see, looking away over the water, was a kind of dull line—that was the woods on t'other side; you couldn't make nothing else out; then a pale place in the sky; then more paleness spreading around; then the river softened up away off, and warn't black any more, but gray; you could see little dark spots drifting along ever so far away— trading scows, and such things; and long black streaks—rafts; sometimes you could hear a sweep screaking; or jumbled-up voices, it was so still, and sounds come so far; and by and by you could see a streak on the water which you know by the look of the streak that there's a snag there in a swift current which breaks on it and makes that streak look that way; and you see the mist curl up off of the water, and the east reddens up, and the river, and you make out a log cabin in the edge of the woods, away on the bank on t'other side of the river, being a woodyard, likely, and piled by them cheats so you can throw a dog through it anywheres; then the nice breeze springs up, and comes fanning you from over there, so cool and fresh and sweet to smell on account of the woods and the flowers; but sometimes not that way, because they've left dead fish laying around, gars and such and they do get pretty rank; and next you've got the full day, and everything smiling in the sun, and the songbirds just going it!

Mark Twain, *Huckleberry Finn*

The Mississippi River is *almost* as important as the title character in *Huckleberry Finn*. Like Heathcliff and the moors, Huck and the river have much in common. Like the river, Huck is strong, free, and very much a part of nature.

● *Exercises in Describing a Setting*

1. Think of novels and stories you've read in which the setting has either played a major part or at least made a strong impression on you. Why did the setting impress you? Have you ever wanted to visit a place as a result of reading about it?

2. Check through the quotation from *Huckleberry Finn*, listing examples of sensory description and dividing them according to the five senses: sight, sound, smell, taste, and touch. Which sense, if any, is not represented? For which sense did you find the most examples? Which senses do you believe are most important in description?

3. Write at least a one-page description of a place. Choose something you know well—your own room, the classroom, the gym, the cafeteria, the place where you work, a park. Use plenty of visual details, but call on your other senses as well to create impressions of sound, smell, taste, and touch.

● *Keeping the Setting in Its Place*

Setting, as you've seen from some of the examples in this chapter, may be crucial in some novels. Less often does setting achieve such prominence in shorter fiction. As you work with short stories, think of setting—or any lengthy description—as the shrubbery of your writing. Keep it pruned back to stay in its place. Don't let it dominate the more important elements.

● *Exercise in Controlling the Setting*

Write single-sentence descriptions setting the scene in terms of both time and place for five different stories. You may want to refer to the one-sentence examples at the beginning of this chapter.

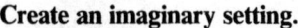

Create an imaginary setting.

● *The Here and Now of Fiction*

If you have ever been caught up in a story, you know what it's like to feel that the events of the story are real. Some writers are more successful than others in pulling the reader into the action of the story. Those writers create the illusion that the story is happening *here and now*.

Trying to create the here-and-now feeling, beginning writers occasionally insist on writing in the present tense, a difficult thing to do and rarely the right choice. The past tense usually works better for actual story writing.

If you are writing in the past tense and your story is set on the Planet Xrklyn or in New Guinea, how can you possibly make your reader feel that the story is happening here and now? First, don't take your story to your reader, bring your reader into the story. You achieve that magical feat by anchoring your story to a specific time and place. Even if both the time and the place are nonexistent, you can make them "real," make the reader believe in them, by using specific details. For example:

The old woman's room was narrow and dark, with but one small window to it; a lantern stood on the floor and lighted it up dimly. It was all filled with reindeer skins and wolf skins, and with reindeer horn, such as the Lapps use to make their carved buttons and knife-handles, and the air in here was rank and stifling. As soon as they were in, the woman turned to Simon, took hold of his head, and with her crooked fingers parted his hair and combed it down in Lapp fashion. She clapped a Lapp cap on him and stood back to glance at him. "Sit down on my stool, now," she said. "But first take out your knife." She was so commanding in voice and manner that the boy could not but choose to do as she told him; he sat down on the stool, and he could not take his eyes off her face, which was flat and brown, and as if smeared with dirt in its net of fine wrinkles.

Isak Dinesen, "The Sailor-Boy's Tale"

The room may be like none you have ever entered; but the author makes you see, feel, hear, smell the setting. Through sensory detail, you are there with Simon. **That** is the here and now of fiction.

● *Exercise in Using Sensory Detail*

Avoid talking about *how* a thing tastes or smells or feels. You can strengthen your writing by naming a sensory stimulus and allowing the reader to react to the image: "I bit into a lemon." "Before we went into the theater, Tom bought hot, buttered popcorn." "Reaching for the limb above, my hand closed on a caterpillar."

If you know the taste of a lemon, the smell of the popcorn, the feel of a caterpillar, the word alone will bring back the sensation. Write five sentences for each of the five senses (twenty-five sentences in all). For example:

Sight   — A cardinal joined the bluejays on the snow-covered bird-feeder hanging from the bare branch.
Sound — "Listen to me," screeched Miss Melson, stamping her foot.
Smell — As soon as she picked up his knapsack, Tommy's mother knew he had found and then forgotten another clam from the beach.
Touch — The cool wind on my face didn't make up for the pain as the sand burned my bare feet.
Taste — I licked my lips and found them coated by the salt spray of the ocean.

● *Writing with the Senses*

1. Make a sketch of the neighborhood where you live, or of a place where you previously lived. You don't need to be able to draw. Label items of importance to you. Like this—

    the creek = = = = = = = = = = = = = = = = = =

                      the   cccccccccccccccccc
                   corn field cccccccccccccccccccc

                      the pond   oooooo

    XX   my   my   XX
    XXXX   aunt's house   x the shed   house   XXXX

    Keep your plan simple enough to transfer to the chalkboard. Be prepared to share a childhood adventure that took place in the area you've outlined.

2. Write a description of the location you've sketched. Include sights, sounds, tastes, smells, and feelings associated with the neighborhood you've described. Remember to name the source of each sensation rather than describe it.

— CHAPTER 6 —

Advancing Scene by Scene:
You Can See It Happening

A scene is a scene by virtue of happening at one time and in one place. It may be one paragraph or many paragraphs long. Each time you move to another place or to a new time you have changed scenes. Not only can you reveal time and place, you may also use scenes to present information, reveal theme, show character, advance the plot, or establish a mood or emotion. You can immediately improve your fiction writing by thinking of your story as a series of scenes and giving your full attention to developing each one.

Each scene in a story should have a purpose: 1) provide background information, 2) reveal character, or 3) move the story forward. Just as every story has a beginning, middle, and end, so does each scene within the story.

Suppose you want to write about Jim, a student who is dreading a meeting with someone who has threatened to beat him up. Your first scene might take place after school with Jim talking over the situation with a friend. A second scene might bring the opponent into the story for a quick introduction and to increase the tension. The opponent repeats his threat and promises to meet Jim before school the next day. The next scene (or possibly the next two) might take place at Jim's home, where the normal everyday life that is going on around the main character contrasts with the worry and fear

Jim faces his opponent.

inside him. An early morning scene or two might be our transition to the climax. The climax would occur when Jim meets the student who plans to beat him up. A final scene after the confrontation will wind up the story.

● *Use Scenes for Pacing the Story*

A common mistake for beginning writers is to try to tell everything at once—with no scene development at all. Here is the conclusion of one student's story:

John spent all that winter working in the shoe factory, saving money to continue his search for Anne. As soon as he had enough money he bought a plane ticket to Switzerland, but he still didn't know where Anne was. All he knew was that her father had sent her to a private school, so he traveled around Switzerland until he finally found the right school.

As soon as he saw Anne, he knew she still loved him. She left the school with him and they were married. They were in Italy by the time her father caught up with them. When he discovered they were already married, he knew he had lost. He accepted his defeat and offered John a job in his company. For a wedding gift, he gave Anne and John a house and a car.

As readers of this passage, we've traveled across oceans, across continents, through several months of time, all in the space of a few lines. We have galloped through time, space, and all sorts of difficulties to reach this happy ending—and we don't believe in it. For one thing, the writer has tried to push a novel's worth of events into one short story. A short story needs a simpler plot, and it must be told scene by scene.

A story is a series of happenings, which should be spelled out in enough detail to make them seem real.

● *Exercise in Analyzing Scenes*

If you are racing forward at the speed of light, you won't have time for dialogue, character, or setting, the elements that bring fiction to life. Note that in both of the examples that follow you have a sense of something happening at a particular moment in a particular place. Examine each of the two scenes to see what details give the moment in the story its sense of reality:

1. From Jack London's *White Fang*:

Henry, squatting over the fire and settling the pot of coffee with a piece of ice, nodded. Nor did he speak till he had taken his seat on the coffin and begun to eat.

"They know where their hides is safe," he said. "They'd sooner eat grub than be grub. They're pretty wise, them dogs."

Bill shook his head. "Oh, I don't know."

His comrade looked at him curiously. "First time I ever heard you say anythin' about their not being wise."

"Henry," said the other, munching with deliberation the beans he was eating, "did you happen to notice the way them dogs kicked up when I was a-feedin' 'em?"

"They did cut up more'n usual," Henry acknowledged.

"How many dogs 've we got, Henry?"

"Six."

"Well, Henry. . . ." Bill stopped for a moment, in order that his words might gain greater significance. "As I was sayin', Henry, we've got six dogs. I took six fish out of the bag. I gave one fish to each dog, an', Henry, I was one fish short."

"You counted wrong."

"We've got six dogs," the other reiterated dispassionately. "I took out six fish. One Ear didn't get no fish. I come back to the bag afterward and got 'm his fish."

"We've only got six dogs," Henry said.

"Henry," Bill went on, "I won't say they was all dogs, but there was seven of 'm got fish."

FOR DISCUSSION: Identify the specifics from the above passage. How do these details make the campfire scene seem like a real experience? How does dialogue help to create a sense of "being there"?

2. From "The Reigate Squires," by Sir Arthur Conan Doyle:

"I hope you are satisfied now?" said Mr. Cunningham, testily.

"Thank you; I think I have seen all that I wished."

"Then, if it is really necessary, we can go into my room."

"If it is not too much trouble."

The J.P. shrugged his shoulders, and led the way into his own chamber, which was a plainly furnished and commonplace room. As we moved across it in the direction of the window, Holmes fell back until he and I were the last of the group. Near the foot of the bed was a small square table, on which stood a dish of oranges and carafe of water. As we passed it, Holmes, to my unutterable astonishment, leaned over in front of me and deliberately knocked the whole thing over. The glass smashed into a thousand pieces, and the fruit rolled about into every corner of the room.

"You've done it now, Watson," said he coolly. "A pretty mess you've made of the carpet."

I stooped in some confusion and began to pick up the fruit, understanding that for some reason my companion desired me to take the blame upon myself. The others did the same, and set the table on its legs again.

"Holloa!" cried the Inspector, "where's he got to?"

Holmes had disappeared.

FOR DISCUSSION: Almost all stories are told in the past tense. As you read, do you think of what is happening as past or present? Why? Look again for details, such as the oranges and the carafe of water. How do these things add to the story? Note the words that reveal Watson's various feelings. What does this information contribute to the story?

● *The Function of the Scene*

Examine the old, simple story below to find the purpose of each scene. The four scenes are numbered to help in your discussion. Notice that the scenes vary in length.

Murder Will Out
by Geoffrey Chaucer

1. Once upon a time and with the best intentions in the world, two comrades set out on a pilgrimage together.

   It happened that they came to a crowded town where there was such a shortage of lodgings that they could not find so much as a cottage where they might both be accommodated together. For this reason they necessarily parted company for the night and each went to his hostelry. One of them was lodged far off in a farmyard, in an oxen stall; the other man—whether by chance or by some decree of that fortune that governs us all—was well provided for.

2. Long before daybreak, the well-lodged of the two comrades dreamed a dream. He dreamed that as he lay in his bed, his friend called upon him and said, "Alas! I shall be murdered tonight as I lie in an oxen stall! Now help me, dear brother, or I die! In all haste, come to me!"

   The dreamer started up out of sleep in fear, but being fully awake, he turned him to sleep again, taking no heed of his dread and considering it but vanity.

   The dream was repeated—with the same result.

   A third time his comrade came to him, as it seemed, and said, "Now I am slain! See my wounds—bloody, deep and wide! Rise up early in the morning, and go to the west gate of the town. There you will see a cart full of dung, in which my body is concealed. Challenge that cart boldly! In truth, it was my gold that caused my death."

   Pale of hue and pitiful of expression, the spirit went on to communicate all the details of the murder.

3. And, you may be sure, the dreamer found that he had dreamed truly.

For in the morning, as soon as it was day, he took his way to his comrade's inn. And as soon as he reached the oxen stall he began to call for his friend.

"Sir," said the innkeeper, "your friend is gone. He left the town at daybreak."

4.   Remembering his dreams, the man could ward off suspicion no longer. Without delay, he proceeded directly to the west gate of the town, where he found a dung cart, ready to go out to manure the land, just as it had been described to him in his dream.

Bold of heart, he began to call for vengeance and justice upon this felony.

"My comrade has been murdered this night, and in this cart his body lies a-gaping. I cry out upon the magistrates who keep and rule this city! Help! Here lies my comrade slain!"

What more shall I add to this tale? The people started up and overturned the cart, and in the midst of the dung they found the dead man newly slain.

QUESTIONS:

(a) Which are the two major scenes in terms of plot? What purposes are served by the other two scenes? Could any scene be left out? Where is the main character in each scene? What time period is covered by each scene?

(b) How could you divide the scenes differently? Could you imagine another scene or two that could be added to expand the story?

(c) The chapter on setting emphasized anchoring the setting in the here-and-now. Chaucer's tale is only loosely tied to the moment. Suggest details that would make each scene of the story more real and more anchored.

EXERCISE: Choose one scene from "Murder Will Out" and rewrite it, supplying sensory details, dialogue, and action to make the scene more real.

● *Variations in Scenes*

An important way to hold the reader's interest is to vary your scenes. Here are some ways to do that:

(a) Funny and serious scenes
(b) Indoor and outdoor scenes
(c) Day and night scenes
(d) Long-time-period and short-time-period scenes
(e) Descriptive and action scenes

What other contrasts could you add to the list?

Vary your scenes.

● *Exercise in Writing a Scene*

Write a single scene, keeping your characters to one time and place and limiting yourself to a single incident. Use dialogue, action, character description, or any means to make the scene real for the reader. If characters talk, if someone frowns or scratches a bug bite or swings a bat at a ball, if nearby objects are named, if something happens in nature, such as a cloud passing over the sun or rain spattering against the window, the moment becomes anchored in time and space. Remember to write in the past tense. Make the scene as vivid as you can.

● *Use Your Imagination*

Choose one of the characters you have developed and imagine that you are that person. Stand like the character. Change your expression to match the character's. Try talking and moving like the character. Now write a scene using details you've collected from this exercise.

● *Organizing by Scenes*

Make a list of scene topics (brief scene descriptions) from a story of your own. Use one you have already written or outline one you plan to write. Put each scene topic on a separate index card or slip of paper. Try rearranging them. Would another order of events work? Look for places to add scenes. Discuss your arrangement with a partner.

—— CHAPTER 7 ——

Beginning and Ending:
A Good Start, A Strong Finish

Opening lines set the tone for the story and introduce your reader to the action.

Here are some ways to capture your reader's attention right from the beginning:

A. Shock or startle.

"Hold your noise!" cried a terrible voice, as a man started up from among the graves at the side of the church porch. "Keep still, you little devil, or I'll cut your throat!"

With these words, Charles Dickens interrupts a quiet churchyard scene, grabbing our attention as well as Pip's in *Great Expectations*.

B. Set a dramatic or exotic scene.

Out there in the cold water, far from land, we waited every night for the coming of the fog, and it came, and we oiled the brass machinery and lit the fog light up in the stone tower.

Ray Bradbury's opening sentence for "The Fog Horn" lets the reader know that something out of the ordinary lies ahead. You may not guess at the fearful monster of the story, but you are prepared for a lonely, eerie experience.

C. Plunge the reader into a dire situation.

I was sick—sick unto death with that long agony; and when they at length unbound me, and I was permitted to sit, I felt that my senses were leaving me. The sentence—the dread sentence of death—was the last of distinct accentuation which reached my ears.

With those words, Edgar Allan Poe pulls us into the horror of "The Pit and the Pendulum."

D. Draw the reader in with a conversational tone, as though you're sitting down to share a story between friends.

It's a story they tell in the border country, where Massachusetts joins Vermont and New Hampshire.

Yes, Dan'l Webster's dead—or at least, they buried him. But every time there's a thunderstorm around Marshfield, they say you can hear his rolling voice in the hollows of the sky.

Stephen Vincent Benét has us settling back to hear a story in the old tradition of the oral tale.

E. Give an immediate glimpse of a character who arouses curiosity.

Filmer Wheeling, lately fifteen, height five feet one inch, weight a hundred and four pounds, and wearing his cherished hard-boiled costume—purplish lumpy trousers, scuffed shoes, and greenish jersey inside out with "39" on the back—felt that Cousin Olita's mind had all gone at last.

Filmer Wheeling's appearance prepares us for the absurdity to follow in Booth Tarkington's "Fame at Fifteen."

● *Exercise in Writing Opening Lines*

1. Look back at some of your favorite novels and short stories. How did they begin? Make your own list of good ways to catch the reader's attention. You may find one that begins with dialogue or one that asks a question or another that begins with fast-paced action or another that starts by making you laugh. Look for variety. Working together as a class, expand the above list.

2. Write an original example for five of the suggested ways to capture your reader's interest. You don't have to follow through by writing an entire story, so you can make your shocking opening as alarming as you can, your unusual setting as exotic as you like. Let your imagination run wild.

● *One Rule for Beginning Stories*

This chapter offers you five examples of ways to begin stories. You can probably think up a dozen more. Remember that you will find many good ways to open a story, and you are free to use them all. Only one first rule applies to the beginning of short stories: **Let the reader know quickly what problem will be the focus of the story**.

● *You Don't Need a Beginning to Begin*

"I have a great story in mind, but I can't write it yet because I don't know how it should begin."

As odd as it sounds, you don't need a beginning to get started writing.

People who wait for the perfect beginning may never write. Write *whatever* you have in mind. Beginnings can come later. Sometimes the opening lines may be the last thing you write. At other times, looking back over what you've written, you may decide that mid-action was the right place to start after all.

● *Bringing the Story to a Conclusion*

One disgusted student claimed that an ending has to be either sad or happy. He was disgusted because he felt that if you didn't want to write a fairy tale, you had to go for the sad ending.

Perhaps a better way to divide endings into two categories is to think of them as either *expected* or *unexpected*.

Do you have to surprise the reader to have a successful story? No, but the story should leave the reader with a large or small sense of discovery.

Unexpected endings with some element of surprise or discovery are desirable. Be careful, however, to see that your conclusion will seem reasonable and believable when the reader thinks back over the story.

A good conclusion should work like a Sherlock Holmes deduction—startle or even amaze at first hearing, but seem perfectly logical on closer examination.

● *Exercise in Working Out a Conclusion*

In a small discussion group, work out a possible ending for each of the plot summaries below. Share ideas with the class to see how others would have resolved the situation:

1. Responding to a newspaper ad, Jason finds himself running strange errands for Mr. Hollister. When he decides his employer is a thief, Jason tries reporting him, only to discover that no one believes any evil of Hollister, a well-known figure in the community. Jason persuades his friend Lynn to help him in a plan to collect evidence. Jason and Lynn are hidden in Mr. Hollister's study while he is talking to a man Jason believes sells stolen goods for Mr. Hollister.

   What happens next?

2. Young Prince Rancon and his pet goat Lawdro have been trapped by an evil wizard. The wizard has stolen the Prince's magic cape, caged Lawdro, and made Prince Rancon into a kitchen drudge. Rancon discovers that the wizard plans to kill Lawdro for use in magic spells. When the wizard locks Rancon in the kitchen one night, the prince realizes he is being kept out of the way so his pet can be killed. Rancon fears for his own life, but he must escape from the stone-walled kitchen, regain his cape, and save Lawdro.

   What does he do?

Prince Rancon and Lawdro

● *Exercise in Writing a Conclusion*

Write an original conclusion to one of the two well-known stories that follow. Remember that a good conclusion shouldn't be too predictable. It should have some element of revelation.

1. Once a lazy but easy-going man named Rip was plagued by a sharp-tongued, nagging wife. To avoid argument—and work—around the house, the man spent most of his time sitting in the village tavern, drinking and talking with other men of the village. Of course, his wife could always find him, and she wasn't above grabbing him by the ear and dragging him back home. When the man needed to escape entirely, he would call his dog, pick up his gun and go hunting in the hills.

   One day in early October, as the man and dog were walking in the hills, they saw a short, old man, struggling with a large keg. Rip offered to help, and without a word, the little man allowed him to take the keg onto his back.

   Over the crest of the hill, Rip and his companion found a clearing where many other little men were gathered. Rip put down the keg and watched as the men played games and drank together. Once in a while, Rip would sneak a drink from the keg, for no one had thanked him for his help or offered him a drink.

   Bored, Rip's dog wandered away. Rip grew tired and fell asleep. When he awoke, he called his dog, but the dog didn't answer. He looked around for his gun but found only a rusty old flintlock in its place.

   Climbing painfully to his feet, he walked slowly back toward town. Coming down the hillside, he was surprised by the sight that lay before him.

2. On a night of celebration in the court of King Arthur, the huge door to the hall where the knights were feasting was flung open. A giant of a knight dressed all in green rode into the room on his horse. When silence fell on the shocked group, the strange knight issued a challenge to any knight who was brave enough to come forward and trade blows with him. The man who accepted the challenge would be allowed to strike the first blow.

   At first all the hall sat in silence. The honor of the court was at stake. Would no one accept the challenge? At last Sir Gawain, youngest knight of all, called out that he would represent the round table and accept the stranger's challenge. After some questioning, his

offer was accepted by King Arthur. Sir Gawain stepped up to the
Green Knight, who dismounted. "You will strike the blow tonight,"
the Green Knight told Gawain, "and one year from this night you
will appear at my castle to be struck by my sword."

Taking careful aim, Sir Gawain swung his sword and cut off the
head of the stranger. Calmly the huge knight stood, picked up his
head, and remounted his horse. Before he rode out, he reminded
Gawain of his bargain.

One year later, after a difficult search, Gawain rode up to the
castle of the Green Knight. Dismounting from his horse, he knocked
on the door.

● *One Rule for Ending Stories*

You are free to create an ending of your choice, whether happy or
sad, expected or unexpected. Just as there is one rule for beginnings,
however, there is also one for endings. The rule is: **Let your major
characters work out the problem (for good or ill, right or wrong)
on their own.**

Remember the young couple who set off on a picnic in Chapter 4?
If Jim Miller has broken his leg falling off his bike, don't send help from
a boat on the lake. Let Elizabeth Overby get Jim back to town, even if
she has to devise a litter and pull him back.

If Elizabeth has been kidnapped, don't have lightning strike the kidnappers. Let Jim, with some assistance from Elizabeth herself, take care
of the rescue.

Once you have devoted most of a story to creating serious difficulties for your characters, don't make the solution to all those problems too
quick or too easy. If your central character is rescued by an accident of
nature or by the arrival of the police or by means of someone older or
stronger, your reader will feel cheated. Tangled webs that suddenly
unravel, puzzles that solve themselves, and characters who are saved
through no effort of their own leave the reader feeling let down.

Of course, good things may happen to your characters. A lost father
can come home, a prize may be won, the sun can shine on a picnic day,
a needed rain may fall in time to save the crops. Just don't let nature or
coincidence solve all the problems.

Problem-solving is the challenge you face as a writer; don't duck the
challenge. With a little planning, you and your characters can provide a
memorable ending for any story.

—— CHAPTER 8 ——

Planning Dialogue:
Let the Characters Say It

Dialogue brings life to a story, helps to reveal character, explains plot elements, and makes a story more readable. Dialogue differs from recorded conversation in having a purpose to serve within the story. Even while it is fulfilling its role in the work of fiction, dialogue should sound natural.

Dialogue is not only good for the story; it's good for you as a writer. When you're stuck for an idea or not sure what should happen next, try letting the characters talk. While you're working out the dialogue, you may discover the key to the next scene.

Examine the examples of dialogue starting on the next page. What purpose does each conversation serve? How is the reader made aware of the distinct personalities of the speakers? Does the dialogue primarily reveal character or plot? Does it add atmosphere? Does it explain a concept? Note that dialogue does not always require full sentences or perfect grammar.

Let the characters talk.

● *Examples of Dialogue*

A. From E. Nesbit's *Five Children and It*:

"You heard those screams?"

"I did think I noticed a sort of something," said Andrew.

"Well, come on then," said the Vicar. "My dear, I *must* go!" He pushed her gently into the sitting-room, banged the door, and rushed out, dragging Andrew by the arm.

A volley of yells greeted them. As it died into silence Andrew shouted, "Hullo, you there! Did you call?"

"Yes," shouted four far-away voices.

"They seem to be in the air," said the Vicar. "Very remarkable."

"Where are you?" shouted Andrew; and Cyril replied in his deepest voice, very slowly and loud:

"CHURCH! TOWER! TOP!"

"Come down, then!" said Andrew; and the same voice replied: *"Can't! Door locked!"*

"My goodness!" said the Vicar. "Andrew, fetch the stable lantern. Perhaps it would be as well to fetch another man from the village."

"With the rest of the gang about, very likely. No sir, if this 'ere ain't a trip—well, may I never! There's cook's cousin at the back door now. He's a keeper, sir, and used to dealing with vicious characters. And he's got his gun, sir."

"Hullo there!" shouted Cyril from the church-tower; "come up and let us out."

"We're a-coming," said Andrew. "I'm a-going to get a policeman and a gun."

"Andrew, Andrew," said the Vicar, "that's not the truth."

"It's near enough, sir, for the likes of them."

FOR DISCUSSION: What characteristics of their speech distinguish the Vicar and Andrew? What clue in this passage suggests that Cyril, and perhaps the others in the church tower, may be young? What elements of humor are in the passage? On the basis of the bit of dialogue here, can you guess the setting of the story?

B. From Rafael Sabatini's *Captain Blood*:

"Are you a doctor?"

"Among other things." The swarthy gentleman continued his study of the patient's pulse. "Firm and regular," he announced at last, and dropped the wrist. "You've taken no great harm."

Don Diego struggled up into a sitting position on the red velvet couch.

"Who the devil are you?" he asked. "And what the devil are you doing in my clothes and aboard my ship?"

The level black eyebrows went up, a faint smile curled the lips of the long mouth.

"You are still delirious, I fear. This is not your ship. This is my ship, and these are my clothes."

"Your ship?" quoth the other, aghast, and still more aghast he added: "Your clothes? But... Then..." Wildly his eyes looked about him. They scanned the cabin once again, scrutinizing each familiar object. "Am I mad?" he asked at last. "Surely this ship is the *Cinco Llagas*?"

"The *Cinco Llagas* it is."

"Then..." The Spaniard broke off. His glance grew still more troubled. "Valga me Dios!" he cried out, like a man in anguish. "Will you tell me also that you are Don Diego de Espinosa?"

"Oh, no, my name is Blood—Captain Peter Blood. This ship, like this handsome suit of clothes, is mine by right of conquest. Just as you, Don Diego, are my prisoner."

FOR DISCUSSION: The two people speaking above are Don Diego and Peter Blood. Identify the speaker of each quotation. What clues do you have? What is the relationship of the two men? What has just happened? What techniques of the author make the revelation of what has occurred more dramatic?

C. From John Masefield's *Midnight Folk*:

"And what do you want now, Mr. Rat?" Kay asked.

"I don't want nothing," Rat said. "Him as thinks as Rat wants anything for doing anything, he'd ought to have the cat after him, and he'd ought to have the dog after him."

"Yes, yes," Kay said, "I'm sure he should."

"Ah," Rat said, "that's what."

"Is there anything that I can do for you, Mr. Rat?" Kay asked.

"Ah," Rat said, "there's many might have asked that question before now, what didn't. Because a fellow is a cellarman and does a bit in the dustbin, and comes a bit close to a old bone now and then (though even that he don't often), people thinks, why, I don't know what they don't think. But what I says is, a fellow is a fellow. You have to come back to that in the end, for all your Tirritts and flurts, and then where are you?"

"Yes, where?" Kay asked, because he didn't know where he was.

"Well, that's what I said, ain't it?" Rat answered in a surly tone. "I thought I'd settled all that once for all."

Kay could not think of anything more to say. He was silent.

"Ah," Rat said, "it's a cruel life is being a cellarman. If I'd my time again, I'd be, I don't what what I'd be, but rather than be a cellarman again, I'd have the cat after me, and I'd have the dog after me, and I'd have . . . I don't know what I wouldn't have after me."

"Is it as bad as that?" Kay said.

"Ah, that's what," Rat said.

"Look here, Mr. Rat," Kay said, "will you have a lump of sugar? It's a bit grubby, but I haven't sucked any of it."

FOR DISCUSSION: How would you describe Rat? (It may help you to know that Kay is an English boy and Rat is indeed a rat.) Would a paragraph of description have worked better here? What does the reader gain by learning about Rat through his own words? What words or expressions does Rat use repeatedly? Do these repetitions contribute to the picture of him? Do you discover anything about the nature of Kay from the above exchange?

D. From Ursula K. Le Guin's *Wizard of Earthsea*:

"What do you call that kind of charm, that made the falcon come?"

"A spell of Summoning."

"Can you call the spirits of the dead to come to you, too?"

He thought she was mocking him with this question, because the falcon had not fully obeyed his summons. He would not let her mock him. "I might if I chose," he said in a calm voice.

"Is it not very difficult, very dangerous, to summon a spirit?"

"Difficult, yes. Dangerous?" He shrugged.

This time he was almost certain there was admiration in her eyes.

"Can you make a love-charm?"

"That is no mastery."

"True," says she, "any village witch can do it. Can you do Changing spells? Can you change your own shape, as wizards do, they say?"

Again he was not quite sure that she did not ask the question mockingly, and so again he replied, "I might if I chose."

FOR DISCUSSION: Without character names, you only know here that a male and female are talking. Who asks the questions and who gives the answers? What do you learn about them both from this conversation?

E. From Madeleine L'Engle's *Swiftly Tilting Planet*:

"What are we going to call her?" Mrs. Murry asked.

Charles Wallace spoke calmly. "Her name is Ananda."

Meg looked at him, but he only smiled slightly. She put the food down and the dog ate hungrily, but tidily.

"Ananda," Mrs. Murry said thoughtfully. "That rings some kind of bell."

"It's Sanskrit," Charles Wallace said.

Meg asked, "Does it mean anything?"

"That joy in existence without which the universe will fall apart and collapse."

"That's a mighty big name for one dog to carry," Mrs. Murry said.

"She's a large dog, and it's her name," Charles Wallace responded.

FOR DISCUSSION: Which of the three characters speaking in this passage defines the Sanskrit name "Ananda"? How do you know? This conversation combines elements of the ordinary and the extraordinary. Find examples of each.

● *Exercises in Writing Dialogue*

1. One problem that arises in writing dialogue is the temptation to make all the characters talk the way the writer does. To help you note the different ways people speak, write down three short conversations that you hear in the next day or two. You may use dialogue you have with someone else or conversations you overhear. Make sure you get four to six changes of speakers in each conversation. Share and discuss these dialogues in class.

2. Find an example of dialogue from fiction and bring it to class for discussion. How does the author of your example make the speakers sound different? What purpose does the dialogue in your example serve?

3. Make a list of expressions you hear people using, including some that you use yourself, expressions such as "Oh, man," "I don't have a clue," "So whatta you say?" and "like" as a sentence starter.

A character needs a distinct voice.

4. Write a one-page dialogue of your own. Decide on a specific situation and limit yourself to two or three speakers. Label the page of dialogue to indicate where the conversation is taking place and what it concerns. For example, "Telephone conversation between friends deciding what to do on Saturday." "Son explaining to his father how the fender was dented on the car." Make the voices of the speakers distinct. Use the conversation to reveal what the characters are like or to convey information to the reader. Keep the responses brief so that you change speakers frequently. Remember that your dialogue should not be a recording of a real conversation. Writers model dialogue on conversation, but use it to make a point efficiently.

5. Present your dialogue to the class. Work with partners or change your voice to represent the changes in speakers.

CHAPTER 9

Choosing a Point of View:
Whose Story Is It?

The narrator provides the point of view for a story. The person telling the story and the storyteller's relation to the action are crucial in shaping the narrative. Broadly speaking, you have a choice between a first-person narrator, the "I" of the story, and a third-person narrator, the storyteller who doesn't appear in the story.

If a character is telling his own story, as Robinson Crusoe or Huck Finn does, the technique is called first-person narration. If the story is told by someone who doesn't appear in the narrative, as *Gone With the Wind* and most O. Henry stories are, the technique is called third-person, or omniscient, narration.

● *First-Person Narration*

Examine the following examples of first-person narratives to find advantages and disadvantages of this point of view.

A. From *Portrait of Jennie*, by Robert Nathan:

There is such a thing as hunger for more than food, and that was the hunger I fed on. I was poor, my work unknown; often without meals, cold, too, in winter in my little studio on the West Side. But that was the least of it.

When I talk about trouble, I am not talking about cold and hunger. There is another kind of suffering for the artist which is worse than anything a winter, or poverty, can do; it is more like a winter of the mind, in which the life of his genius, the living sap of his work, seems frozen and motionless, caught—perhaps forever—in a season of death; and who knows if spring will ever come again.

B. From *David Copperfield*, by Charles Dickens:

Whether I shall turn out to be the hero of my own life, or whether that station will be held by anybody else, these pages must show. To begin my life with the beginning of my life, I record that I was born (as I have been informed and believe) on a Friday, at twelve o'clock at night. It was remarked that the clock began to strike, and I began to cry, simultaneously.

FOR DISCUSSION: First-person narratives have a strong appeal for most readers. Why do you think this is so? What do you gain by telling a story in the first person? What are the disadvantages? (Our second example illustrates one obvious disadvantage. Can you think of others?) What did you learn about each of the narrators above? If you were going to write a first-person story, how could you reveal the narrator's appearance and character to the readers?

● *Third-Person Narration*

Note how the following examples of third-person narratives below differ in tone from the first-person examples.

A. From Enid Bagnold's *National Velvet*:

"Take a radish, Velvet."

"Couldn't bite a *radish*!"

"Go without then," said Mr. Brown happily, and leant back to light his pipe.

All the Browns tilted their chairs. Nobody ever told them it would hurt the carpet. They ate, ruminated, and tilted. Only Mrs. Brown sat solid and silent. She did not talk much, but managed the till down at the shop in the street. She knew all about courage and endurance, to the last ounce of strength, from the first swallow of overcome timidity. She valued and appraised each daughter, she knew what each daughter could do.

B. From "An Occurrence at Owl Creek Bridge," by Ambrose Bierce:

A man stood upon a railroad bridge in northern Alabama, looking down into the swift water twenty feet below. The man's hands were behind his back, the wrists bound with a cord. A rope closely encircled his neck. It was attached to a stout cross-timber above his head and the slack fell to the level of his knees. Some loose boards laid upon the sleepers supporting the metals of the railway supplied a footing for him and his executioners—two private soldiers of the Federal army, directed by a sergeant who in civil life may have been a deputy sheriff. At a short remove upon the same temporary platform was an officer in the uniform of his rank, armed. He was a captain. A sentinel at each end of the bridge stood with his rifle in the position known as "support," that is to say, vertical in front of the left shoulder, the hammer resting on the forearm thrown straight across the chest—a formal and unnatural position, enforcing an erect carriage of the body. It did not appear to be the duty of these two men to know what was occurring at the center of the bridge; they merely blockaded the two ends of the foot planking that traversed it.

FOR DISCUSSION: A first-person story draws us immediately into the action and into identifying with a character. How can an omniscient narrator engage our interest? Why is a third-person narrator better for a story that will concern a group of people rather than an individual? In the second example, the main character is about to be executed. How would having him serve as a first-person narrator destroy the suspense of the story? What other advantages can you gain by using a third-person narrator? In one type of third-person narrative, the narrator knows and reveals the thoughts and feelings of the characters. In a second type of third-person narrative, the narrator tells the story as an external observer. Which of the passages above illustrates the omniscient narrator with knowledge of thoughts and feelings? Which illustrates the limited third-person narrator who is looking on from the outside?

● *Exercise in Using Point of View*

Read through the passage quoted below. Then quickly rewrite all three paragraphs, allowing Della to tell the story in the first person.

From "The Gift of the Magi," by O. Henry:

One dollar and eighty-seven cents. That was all. And sixty cents of it was in pennies. Pennies saved one and two at a time by bulldozing the grocer and vegetable man and the butcher until one's cheeks burned with the silent imputation of parsimony that such close dealing implied. Three times Della counted it. One dollar and eighty-seven cents. And the next day would be Christmas.

There was clearly nothing to do but flop down on the shabby little couch and howl. So Della did it. Which instigates the moral reflection that life is made up of sniffles, and smiles, with sniffles predominating.

While the mistress of the house is gradually subsiding from the first stage to the second, take a look at the home. A furnished flat at $8 per week. It did not exactly beggar description, but it certainly had that word on the lookout for the mendicancy squad.

FOR DISCUSSION: Which of these three paragraphs was the most difficult to transpose from third to first person? Did you gain anything by making the change? Does this section sound better or worse? With careful work, the changes should result in a passage not much different in effect from the original. O. Henry might have told this part of the story just as well using a first-person narrator. Can you guess at what may be coming in the story that would make third-person more desirable?

● *Limited First-Person Narrator*

The examples of first-person narration you examined above represent the most common use of first-person narrator, that is, someone who actively participates in the story being told. A second type of narrator who appears as "I" in a story, however, introduces the action and withdraws to relate the story from a distance.

A. From "What the Old Man Does Is Always Right," by Hans Christian Andersen:

I will tell you the story which was told to me when I was a little boy. Every time I thought of the story, it seemed to me to become more and more charming; for it is with stories as it is with many people—they become better as they grow older.

B. From Joseph Conrad's "Heart of Darkness":

Between us there was, as I have already said somewhere, the bond of the sea. Besides holding our hearts together through long periods of separation, it had the effect of making us tolerant of each other's yarns—and even convictions. The Lawyer—the best of old fellows—had, because of his many virtues, the only cushion on deck, and was lying on the only rug. The Accountant had brought out already a box of dominoes, and was toying architecturally with the bones. Marlow sat cross-legged right aft, leaning against the mizzen-mast. He had sunken cheeks, a yellow complexion, a straight back, an ascetic aspect, and, with his arms dropped, the palms of hands outwards, resembled an idol.

FOR DISCUSSION: In the first instance the narrator relates a story he has heard from someone else. He appears to speak directly to the reader. In the second instance, the narrator is not so much retelling a story as recounting the evening on which he heard the story; he introduces Marlow, a second narrator to tell the tale. What effect does a storyteller character within the story have on you? Do you feel more or less drawn to the story? Why?

Some narrators tell stories they have heard from someone else.

● *Analyzing Point of View*

Choose a story you have read recently and answer the following questions.

1. Who tells the story?
2. How much does the narrator know?

3. How do you learn about the narrator? (You may learn about a first-person narrator from action, description, dialogue, the narrator's own statements, or other characters' statements. On the other hand, you may read through an entire story without learning anything about a third-person narrator.)

4. Is the narrator a participant in the action or just an observer?

5. Imagine the story told from a different point of view. How would it be changed?

● *Point of View as a Writing Technique*

Sometimes you can save a story that isn't working by changing the point of view. If your story is in the third person, it may need a first-person narrator to narrow the focus and humanize the story. Or perhaps you need to replace your first-person narrator with an omniscient one to give that narrator freedom to see and know more than any individual in the story could.

1. Use the instructions in this exercise to put yourself in the place of someone whose point of view is (or was) in opposition to your own. Complete both (a) and (b).

   (a) Write a paragraph describing an argument or disagreement you have had. The dispute may be as recent or as far in the past as you like. Present the disagreement from your own point of view, making as strong a case as you can for yourself. (Have you ever been falsely accused of something or blamed for an accident without being given a chance to explain, or do you have a lifelong tendency to argue with one particular family member?) Try to recall a good complex conflict.

   (b) Now go back to the argument you described from your own point of view above and rewrite the incident presenting the case from the other person's viewpoint. Try to put yourself in the other person's place and make the best argument that individual could advance on his or her own behalf.

2. Pick one of the story ideas that follow and write two segments, changing viewpoint as directed.

(a) Two friends have discovered a wallet with more than a thousand dollars in it. Write a page from the point of view of one who wants to keep the money. Next, write a page from the point of view of a first-person narrator who insists on advertising for the real owner of the wallet. (Note that these paragraphs should not be simply dialogue or argument between the two. Put yourself inside the head of first one friend and then the other.)

(b) Writing first from an omniscient point of view, supply the beginning paragraphs of a story about a soldier who has been asked to take a message on a grueling run across the hills through enemy lines. Next, write a new beginning, speaking in the first person as the running soldier.

(c) Imagine that a detective in disguise is pursuing a criminal who is also in disguise. Write three paragraphs describing a meeting between the two, first using a third-person limited narrator *who does not know which is which*. Next, rewrite these paragraphs, narrating in the first person as the character of your choice.

A soldier's story

CHAPTER 10

Varying the Form:
Mystery, Fantasy and Science Fiction, Humor, and Ghost Stories

The structure or framework of short fiction is basically the same regardless of your subject matter, but some stories call for special elements. Here are a few variations to give you practice in working with different types of stories.

Try to think of each plot idea as your own, and discuss with the group how you would develop the story. If you decide to write a short story from one of the suggestions, note that you usually will have to supply the characters. Even for the main character, you may choose age, sex, and personality details. Changing the characters will dramatically change each story.

• *Mystery Stories*

While mysteries usually involve crime, they can also concern puzzles that do not originate from wrongdoing. They may include searches for lost objects or for people who have disappeared even when no crime was involved.

Typically, a mystery story poses a question: Who stole the diamonds? Where is the missing will? Why did the professor set his wet boots inside the house and then walk away? What happened to the medieval tapestry that was shipped from Venice but never arrived in New York?

Mysteries make frequent use of detectives, amateur or professional, as main characters. Clues are discovered. Finally, a satisfying answer to the major question of the story is required for the ending.

Examine the suggested mystery plots that follow and decide how you would handle each story.

Mystery Plots

1. A famous painting at a local museum is identified as a forgery. The real painting was known to be there a week ago when an art expert examined it. Since then it has been guarded constantly. When and how was the real painting taken and the substitution made?

2. Your sleuth is on an island vacation with a friend when the friend disappears. Apparently the disappearance is a kidnapping, but no one on the island knew the two friends. The two had only met the hotel personnel, the manager of a fishing-boat charter service, and the guide who toured the island with them on the first day. Who would kidnap the friend? Why? What has happened?

3. Your main character is forced into the role of sleuth after he or she picks up the wrong piece of luggage at the airport baggage claim. Someone is prepared to use violence to get the suitcase back. Your character would gladly return it and take his or her own in its place, but the pursuer won't stop to talk. What is in the suitcase? What does your character do?

4. Several buildings in town have burned under suspicious circumstances. The police believe an arsonist is at work. Your sleuth has noticed that each burned building is next door to a bank. No bank robberies have been reported, but the sleuth thinks the problem may be something more than arson alone. What is the significance of all the burned buildings being located next to banks? What does the sleuth do?

5. Your sleuth is searching for a master criminal known only as the Colonel, who has been involved in many crimes and is also known to head a counterfeiting ring. Your sleuth tries to join the counterfeiting ring to find out who the Colonel is. What happens?

● *Fantasy and Science Fiction*

Fantasy is the larger category, including all stories with incredible or unreal elements, imaginary countries, characters with strange powers, or scientific inventions that don't really exist. Science fiction in particular focuses on adventures on other planets, in other worlds, in the future, or involving as yet undiscovered or nonexistent scientific principles.

The next series of suggested plots is a mix of fantasy and science fiction. Which ones stir your imagination? How would you develop the plots?

Fantasy and S.F. Plots

1. Time is behaving strangely, moving too quickly for some people and too slowly for others. Your main character is investigating what appears to be a change in the earth's magnetic poles. Has he or she found the solution to the mystery, or is it more complicated? Why and how has the earth's magnetism altered?

2. In the land of Llyr, great danger lurks. A wizard has frozen most of the land, and the ice is slowly covering everything. The only hope for the people of Llyr lies in a long-lost source of heat. Perhaps the heat source is only an old tale, but your main character knows he or she can only find out by locating the last living descendant of Methryn, Llyr's final Custodian of Oral History, a man who lived more than a century earlier. Methryn, of course, is gone, but perhaps his young relative will know the old stories. How does your main character set about finding this person?

3. On the planet Cordrum, Bayle and Mellyn, who are brother and sister, are orphans in a world where the Magalons rule. The Magalons are tiger-like creatures of great intelligence and equally great cruelty, who took over the planet from the parents of Bayle and Mellyn, who must take control again or see their people become slaves in the mines beneath the glacier fields. What do they do?

4. A fire has broken out in the engine room of the spaceship *Paragona*, where one young officer is alone. Dracco, the captain of the spaceship, has just spotted a deadly enemy, the spaceship *Condor*. All of the *Paragona*'s other crew members are concentrating on the coming attack. What does the young officer do? With trouble inside and out, how will the *Paragona* survive?

Captain Dracco's adventure

5. Professor Pendrith has invented a remarkable machine. The government will pay him or her to destroy the machine, but the criminal underworld is determined to have it, either by paying the professor a fabulous sum, or by stealing it from him or her. What does the machine do? The criminals want this machine so badly that the professor's life is in danger. What does he or she do?

● *Humor*

Humor is an important part of any writing. You may introduce a touch of comedy through a joke, gag, or riddle, through a comic character, or through a pun or play on words. Occasional humor can be introduced even into serious stories.

To write a story that is primarily humorous usually requires a comic situation. Often such situations rely on mistaken identities, an accumulation of errors, unexpected meetings, a pairing of opposites, or placing characters in unlikely situations.

No matter how great or small your talent for comedy may be, you can increase your skill at comedy writing through practice. See what you would do with the situations below. Remember that sometimes the only difference between tragedy and comedy is the author's attitude toward the material. Allow yourself to think of exaggerations and even ridiculous complications that might add to the humor.

Comic Situations

1. Mrs. Gardener leaves a message for her older daughter asking her to cook dinner for an important guest who will be coming to visit that evening. Mrs. Gardener will be at work too late to cook the meal or clean the house. Sam and Mandy, the younger children in the family, are the only ones at home, however. To help out, they decide to follow through on the request for a "company dinner" on their own.

2. A big-city family buys a farm to try country life. The farm is also home to goats, geese, a few chickens, and some cows. The family has enthusiasm for their new life, but not much experience. The setting, the chores, the animals are all foreign to the family members, who find that as soon as they solve one problem, another crops up.

3. A youngster decides to take home a stray cat, even though cats are forbidden in his or her house. He or she hides the cat while asking permission to keep it. When the parents reject the possibility of a pet, the main character tries to keep the cat a secret until either a home can be found for it or it can be safely introduced to the resisting parents.

4. Two characters who have a longstanding feud are given the lead roles in a play. Each wants to stay in the play but get rid of the other. Efforts at sabotaging each other constantly backfire.

5. A nearsighted person who refuses to wear glasses adopts a pig, believing it's an overweight, not-very-attractive dog.

● *Ghost Stories*

Ghost stories, really another subdivision of fantasy, have been around as long as people have been telling stories. Their only true requirements are an eerie atmosphere and some experience that cannot be accounted for in the ordinary world. Don't overlook the possibility of ghosts that aren't necessarily people. Buildings, animals, and other non-human ghosts also make appearances in fiction.

Test your imagination on the following plot ideas.

Try your hand at a ghost story.

Ghost Story Plots

1. A bell that sounded a warning for a New England town during the American Revolution has hung silent for more than two centuries. Making a nighttime visit to fulfill a dare, a student enters the museum that houses the bell. To prove he or she has been inside, the student must ring the bell long enough for his or her friends to hear it outside. The tolling of the long-silent bell brings back an army of British soldiers. What happens to the student and the student's friends?

2. An old mirror bought at a pawnshop reflects scenes from the past whenever it's exposed to candlelight. What is seen in the mirror? What happens to the family or individual who has bought the mirror?

3. While remodeling an old house, the Morgan family uncovers a sealed-up fireplace. The mantel as well as other parts of the fireplace are made of marble, and the family is proud of the discovery until they find that the fireplace is haunted. How and why would a ghost be associated with a fireplace?

4. Spending the night in an old inn, the main character wakes up and wanders into a long, candlelit wing of the house where he or she sees a strange collection of guests. At last, the main character finds his or her assigned bedroom and falls asleep again until morning. The next day the guest learns that the wing, which opened off the end of his or her own hallway, did once exist but was destroyed many years ago. What is the secret of the haunted inn?

5. A house appears to be haunted by a cat that gets in and out even when all the doors are locked and the windows closed. The cat causes no disturbance except for its habit of sitting halfway up the stairs. Can you explain the cat?

● *Finding a Style of Your Own*

Many options are available to you for framing the events of a short story and making them exciting for the reader. Which story type covered in this chapter suited you best? Perhaps you found more than one you want to continue using. As you write, you will develop your own style and find the kind of storytelling that you do well and enjoy most.

● *Writing Exercise*

Write three plot ideas for one or more of the story types discussed in this chapter. Talk over your ideas in class. Then choose one to expand into a short story. As you write your story, remember to catch the reader's interest early, develop your characters, build interest in the plot, and bring the story to a credible conclusion.

— CHAPTER 11 —

Improving Your Writing Skills: *Activities for the Writer*

Your ability as a writer will grow in proportion to the amount of time you devote to writing. Not all writing time will—or should—contribute to a finished story. Some of the activities in this chapter get you started on a story; others offer you a chance to increase your creativity, to work independently on improving your writing, or to work with others on a writing project.

Creative writing is an exciting undertaking, involving challenges, fun, discovery, and sharing. The exhilaration of creating your own world and commanding your reader's attention more than compensates for the work involved.

As you work through this chapter, note the activities you like best. You can return to them for continued exercise in writing techniques.

● *Exercises*

1. Consider each of the following opening lines. Which would attract your attention? Why? Explain why you are not interested in the others.

It happened that green and crazy summer when Frankie was twelve years old. This was the summer when for a long time she had not been a member. She belonged to no club and was a member of nothing in the world. Frankie had become an unjoined person who hung around in doorways, and she was afraid.

Carson McCullers, *The Member of the Wedding*

"Holmes," said I, as I stood one morning in our bow-window looking down the street, "here is a madman coming along. It seems rather sad that his relatives should allow him to come out alone."

Sir Arthur Conan Doyle, "The Beryl Coronet"

He was born with a gift of laughter and a sense that the world was mad.

Rafael Sabatini, *Scaramouche*

Scarlett O'Hara was not beautiful, but men seldom realized it when caught by her charm as the Tarleton twins were.

Margaret Mitchell, *Gone With the Wind*

Brrrrrrriiiiiiiiiiiiiiiiiiinng!
An alarm clock clanged in the dark and silent room. A bed spring creaked. A woman's voice sang out impatiently:
   "Bigger, shut that thing off!"

Richard Wright, *Native Son*

When I was a young boy, if I was sick or in trouble, or had been beaten at school, I used to remember that on the day I was born my father had wanted to kill me.

Mary Renault, *The Last of the Wine*

I had this story from one who had no business to tell it to me, or to any other.

Edgar Rice Burroughs, *Tarzan of the Apes*

Martha Pym said that she had never seen a ghost and that she would very much like to do so, "particularly at Christmas, for you can laugh as you like, that is the correct time to see a ghost."

Marjorie Bowen, "The Crown Derby Plate"

Mother died today. Or, maybe, yesterday; I can't be sure. The telegram from the Home says: YOUR MOTHER PASSED AWAY. FUNERAL TOMORROW. DEEP SYMPATHY. Which leaves the matter doubtful; it could have been yesterday.

Albert Camus, *The Stranger*

---

2. Someone has said, "Fiction should always tell the truth." Explain in your own words what that statement means.

3. Identify a talisman in your life, some object that arouses a strong emotion. It might be a picture of the dog that died when you were ten, or it might be your lucky coin. Or, it may not be an object at all. It could be a song or a place. Now try explaining to someone else what your talisman means to you. Try to make the listener feel the same emotions.

4. Make a list of three or four dire situations that a character might face. Working with a small group of people, discuss ways to make those dire situations even worse.

5. At a separate time from when you do number 4, in a small group discuss ways to rescue characters from those dire situations.

6. Create a character by combining personality traits from three people you know well.

7. Find any fiction you have already written, complete or incomplete, perhaps even something you don't like, and think of two ways you might use that fiction as a part of something larger. Open your mind to creative possibilities on this one.

8. Try writing to music. Some people like a musical background; others don't. Try varying the type of music you listen to and its volume. Do you write better to music? Is it easier or harder to come up with ideas? Does the change in the type of music affect what you write?

9. Find an observation post and spend thirty to forty minutes recording what you see, hear, feel—everything you experience.

Try writing to music.

10. Write an account of a favorite family story that does not directly involve you. If you don't have such a story, ask a relative to tell you a remembered incident from his or her childhood.

11. Make a list of three possible villains. Include a name, occupation, physical description, and major personality traits. Which of the villains appeals to you most? Why? What sort of story would suit this villain?

12. Try a ten-minute writing session. Pick up or look at a nearby object. Whatever comes to hand will do. Write about the object as rapidly and as steadily as you can for ten minutes. Use an alarm clock or have someone else time you and call a halt so you won't waste time checking your watch. What you write may be mostly uninteresting, but look for a good line or a good phrase.

13. Create the "skeleton" of a mystery story. Describe your sleuth, choose a crime, and decide on a criminal and additional suspects. Should your sleuth have an assistant? If so, include a description of him or her.

14. What qualities do you appreciate most in a hero? Make up your own list and then compare it with others. Rank your list of characteristics, deciding which ones are most important to you.

15. Describe a character who possesses all the qualities you value most. Include background and physical appearance to make the character real.

16. Create a setting for a fantasy. Use details from the real world, but add touches from your imagination that add up to a time, a place, or a society like nothing in this world.

17. Make a list of problems or situations that would grab your attention in a story. Imagine these are situations you've chosen to read about rather than write about.

18. Remember that stories are made of these basics:

    (a) Characters in a particular situation

    (b) Problems that complicate the situation

    (c) A resolution to the situation

    Using that sequence, supply information for a short story.

19. Write an opening paragraph for a story, and then trade with another student. You agree either to finish the story or to continue to trade after each person has contributed a paragraph or two.

20. Describe some traumatic incident from your early childhood, something that hurt you, made you angry, made you cry. Make the incident so real that the reader experiences your feelings.

21. In a quest story you have a character in search of something, just as the Knights of the Round Table went in search of the Holy Grail. Make a list of five things that could serve as the goal of a quest. Note that a quest might be a search for something intangible, such as an identity for an amnesiac or the solution to a mystery. Try to include some real objects and some intangibles in your list.

22. Write accounts of a single incident from two different points of view: parent and child, teacher and student, younger brother and older sister, male and female, doctor and patient. Come up with your own pair of characters; put them together in a scene that we see first from one point of view and then from the other. Try to put yourself into each character and shift your views to suit the featured individual.

23. Creating your own headline, write a story of the sort that might appear in one of the tabloid newspapers you see in the supermarket, under headlines such as "Child Raised by Aliens Returns to His Parents," "Bigfoot Seen in Camden, New Jersey," or "Newborn Baby Speaks Dutch."

24. Write a brief dream sequence, using either a dream you have really had or drawing on your imagination. Now describe the character who had the dream.

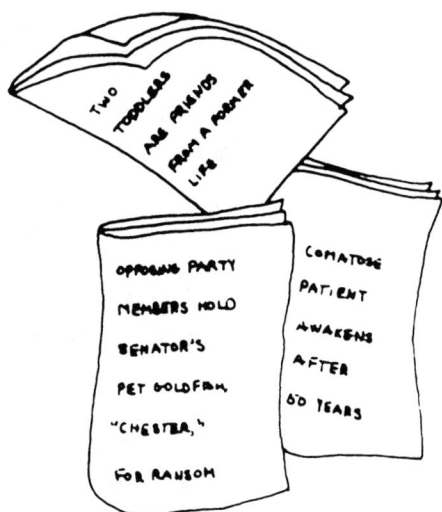

Write your own amazing headline.

25. Using the information you developed in number 24, complete a story that begins "Each time I began to think I was finally rid of the dream, it would come back again. The same things happening over and over, in the same way."

26. Write a scene from the point of view of a blindfolded character. Without directly stating the reason for the blindfold, be sure the reader can understand why it is there.

27. Choose some stranger you see in public during the next week and make mental notes about the person's appearance—hair, clothing, features, posture, expression—every fact you can remember. As soon as possible write a point-by-point description. Share these in class so that you can compare the number and kind of details you saw with those noted by others.

28. You may have been told to "write about what you know," but it is also all right to go and find out about something and then write about it. Obtain a list of rules for a game. It could be a sport, a children's party game, a card game, a board game or any other. Go over the list of rules until you understand them. How could you incorporate this game into a story? Write a summary of the story.

● *Stories to Write*

The following activities are story-writing assignments. Some will appeal to you more than others, but you should try them all. Don't expect every story to be a success. Through a variety of writing assignments, you may discover an unexpected talent.

1. Choose one of your story ideas and write it in the form of a one-act play. Check your dialogue activities to find a possible starting point.

2. Write a narrative poem. Notice that in poetry you may lose much of the description in the story. The plot may become both compressed and stark.

3. Tell a story in the form of a comic strip. For this, you need a clear, uncomplicated storyline. Think of your story in scenes and work with simple pictures.

4. Write a story as a radio script. A radio script is much like a play, except that you must rely only on sound.

5. Write a short mystery that includes a sleuth, a crime, and suspects. A master villain is optional, but you will need a criminal of some sort.

Try the suggestions above several times to find your favorites. Remember that there is more than one form in which to tell a story, more than one way to use a story idea.

— CHAPTER 12 —

Writing the Story:
Fifteen Story Assignments

This chapter contains fifteen writing assignments with suggestions to get you started on each story. Not every writer wants to pursue every type of story, but for beginners a wide variety of experience is essential.

Be bold in trying new approaches.

1. Edith List, who wrote numerous short stories and poems, as well as radio and television scripts, got her start with a short story written as an assignment in a high school class when she was seventeen years old. Her task was to take the bare facts of a newspaper report and turn them into a short story. She chose an article about an automobile accident that resulted in the deaths of five teenagers. To transform the scant information of the account into a story, she introduced a teenage narrator who not only witnesses the accident but assists in pulling the bodies of the victims out of a river. She called her story, "Joy Ride."

    Make a collection of newspaper articles that could serve as the subjects for short stories. Select one and write a short story of your own. Remember that you are not a reporter, so you have no obligation to stick to the original outline of events.

2. Choose a familiar fairy tale and rewrite it as a contemporary story. You may want to use the one worked with in Chapter 2, or you may choose a different one. Update the setting and change details as needed.

3. Make a collection of your favorite jokes from television, newspapers, magazines, or movies. From your assortment, pick the dozen best. Now think of a plot that will allow you to include all twelve and write a story that features them.

4. Write a story centering on an overheard conversation. You might have a character eavesdrop on a conversation believing that it is about him or her, when in reality it concerns someone else. You might have your main character overhear one side of a telephone conversation and jump to a mistaken conclusion about what is being discussed. Or, the overheard conversation may not be misunderstood; it may instead reveal a painful or startling piece of information to the one who overhears it.

5. In his story "By the Waters of Babylon," Stephen Vincent Benét immerses his reader in a strange world, where civilization is just returning after massive destruction. Examine the beginning of his story:

> The north and the west and the south are good hunting ground, but it is forbidden to go east. It is forbidden to go to any of the Dead Places except to search for metal, and then he who touches the metal must be a priest or the son of a priest. Afterwards, both the man and the metal must be purified. These are the rules and the laws; they are well made. It is forbidden to cross the great river and look upon the place that was the Place of the Gods—this is most strictly forbidden. We do not even say its name though we know its name. It is there that spirits live, and demons—it is there that there are the ashes of the Great Burning. These things are forbidden—they have been forbidden since the beginning of time.
>
> My father is a priest; I am the son of a priest. I have been in the Dead Places near us, with my father—at first I was afraid. When my father went into the house to search for metal, I stood by the door and my heart felt small and weak. It was a dead man's house, a spirit house. It did not have the smell of man, though there were old bones in a corner. But it is not fitting that a priest's son should show fear. I looked at the bones in the shadow and kept my voice still.

Write your own story of a few survivors struggling to form a new way of life. The disaster within your story may be global or more local, like the sinking of a ship or the flooding of a town.

6. Spend some class time identifying and discussing ethical problems, such as having to choose between telling the truth and sparing someone's feelings, or between assuming responsibility for what was an accident or keeping quiet since you didn't intend it to happen. Discuss such questions as "Would you admit your own guilt to save a friend from being blamed for something you did?" and "Would you accept the blame to save someone who wasn't a friend?"

   Focusing on a single event that serves to reveal the true nature of the central character, write a short story about an ethical dilemma. In writing your story, use action and dialogue to make a hidden strength or weakness of the character clear to the reader.

7. Using a limited third-person point of view, relate a memorable incident from your childhood, making yourself the central character. Interweave imaginary details with reality for plot.

8. Holidays are often filled with tension as well as joy. Have you ever experienced a disastrous birthday? Given a gift that turned out to be a mistake? Embarrassed yourself or your family in front of a large gathering? Base a story on a holiday celebration in your family. Use details from real life to enrich the story, but feel free to elaborate and embellish reality to come up with a plot.

9. Choose one of the three situations below and develop your own story to fit it:

   (a) Write a short story about arriving as a tourist on a distant planet.

   (b) Write a comic story about a series of mishaps that occur during a school's science fair.

   (c) Write a story about a camping trip during which people and wildlife clash.

10. Choose a narrative poem or a poem about a character (Edgar Lee Masters's *Spoon River Anthology* is one good source) and rewrite the poem as a short story, remembering to develop scenes and include dialogue. You have the option of working with something as light as "The Cremation of Sam McGee" or as serious as "Richard Cory."

11. Many stories and novels have focused on or included animal characters that add pathos or humor through their similarity or contrast to human behavior. This passage from Jessamyn West's *Friendly Persuasion* introduces the topic of "geese," but the story quickly focuses on just one goose, the wonderful pacing goose named Samantha.

"Eliza, I got tight fences, but the goose's never been hatched that'll admit fences exist. And an old gander'd just as soon go through a fence as hiss—and if he can't find a hole or crack in a fence he'll lift the latch."

"Jess," said Eliza flatly, "thee don't like geese."

"Well," said Jess, 'I wouldn't go so far's to say I didn't like them, but I will say that if there's any meaner, dirtier animal, or one that glories in it more, I don't know it. And a thing I've never been able to understand about thee Eliza is what thee sees in shifty-eyed birds."

"Geese," said Eliza, with a dreaminess unusual to her, "march along so lordly like . . . they're pretty as swans floating down a branch . . . in fall they stretch out their necks and honk to geese passing overhead as if they's wild. My father never had any trouble raising geese and I've heard him say many a time that there's no better food for a brisk morning than a fried goose egg."

Choose one of the following alternatives:
(a) Write a story from the point of view of a pet you have now or have had.
(b) Focus your story on two characters with opposing attitudes toward a particular animal. (c) Create an imaginary animal to serve as a pet in a fantasy story.

Create an imaginary animal character.

12. Stories often begin with a character who, through no fault of his own, is thrust into an unfamiliar situation or even a bizarre new world, as in the case of the unidentified character here:

"Stay out of there!" I yelled at my cousin, but he was off like a dog after a rabbit. Mere words wouldn't stop him.

I set off at a good run myself and was just in time to see his green jacket disappear beyond the cave's opening.

Calling his name, I entered the cool darkness, where I should have stopped to give my eyes time to adjust to the change from the brightness outside. Instead, I tripped and felt myself falling. I don't remember hitting bottom. The first thing I do remember was a group of unearthly looking people bending over me. By the light of the lanterns they carried, I could see the bright glitter of jewels in the walls all around us.

Your character is thrust into a new world.

You may choose either to pick up with the fourth paragraph of this story and develop it as you please, or to create your own sudden transition from the familiar to the unexpected. In either case, write a complete story that shows both what the new situation is and how your character copes with it.

13. In Alfred, Lord Tennyson's *Idylls of the King*, Arthur, together with his knights, establishes the rules that will govern their society of the Round Table:

> I made them lay their hands in mine and swear
> To reverence the King, as if he were
> Their conscience, and their conscience as their king,
> To break the heathen and uphold the Christ,
> To ride abroad redressing human wrongs,
> To speak no slander, no, nor listen to it,
> To honor his own words as if his God's,
> To lead sweet lives in purest chastity,
> To love one maiden only, cleave to her,
> And worship her by years of noble deeds,
> Until they won her.

Make up your own list of rules for a society, group, or gang. Then write a story showing how your society lives by (or fails to live by) its rules.

14. Choose a section from a novel you have read and adapt it as a short story or as a dramatic script for a television play.

15. "The Fifty-First Dragon" by Heywood Broun is the story of an inept young man who would like to be a knight but appears to have little chance of succeeding:

Of all the pupils at the knight school Gawaine le Coeur-Hardy was among the least promising. He was tall and sturdy, but his instructors soon discovered that he lacked spirit. He would hide in the woods when the jousting class was called, although his companions and members of the faculty sought to appeal to his better nature by shouting to him to come out and break his neck like a man. Even when they told him that the lances were padded, the horses no more than ponies, and the field unusually soft for late autumn, Gawaine refused to grow enthusiastic. The Headmaster and the Assistant Professor of Pleasaunce were discussing the case one spring afternoon, and the Assistant Professor could see no remedy but expulsion.

Recall some event in your life that tested your courage without posing a real threat to your life or anyone else's. You might recall your first visit to a Halloween haunted house exhibit, your first ride on a roller coaster, or your first day at school. Write a fictional account of the incident, exaggerating the problems you faced to create a humorous version of a traditional heroic feat.